MW01404535

Abyssal Communion & Rite of Imbibement

Ψ

S. Connolly

Abyssal Communion
&
Rite of Imbibement

Ψ

S. Connolly

DB PUBLISHING 2013

MMXIII

DB Publishing is an arm of Darkerwood Publishing Group, PO Box 2011, Arvada, CO 80001.

ISBN-13:9781494872489

Abyssal Communion & Rite of Imbibement© 2013 by S. Connolly. No part of this book may be reproduced in any form, electronic or other, without express written permission from the author and publisher. Please respect the author's copyright.

Book Design by Kim Anderson and Stephanie Reisner

*May your rites be well attended and may the Daemonic dwell within you all of your days.
Praise Be Sobek, The Blood is the Life!*

Foreword

The Abyssal Communion (also called the Elemental Communion) is a rite in which the dedicant symbolically brings into him/herself all of the elements of creation. In a sense, it is a fluid, moving, elemental balancing ritual that can be included in devotional rites, magickal work, or used alone as a ritual by itself. The timeless beauty and relevance of the ritual makes it extremely popular with both practicing coven/sects and solitary practitioners. It can be performed as a simple and unspoken ritual, or it can be elaborate and ceremonial with the included orations. It can be modified based on your particular pantheon or personal spiritual preferences and incorporated into any personal paradigm and practice.

The Rite of Imbibement is traditionally a Daemonolatry specific ritual often incorporated into the Abyssal Communion. This rite can also be incorporated into any devotional or magickal work and it does not necessarily need to be practiced in conjunction with the Abyssal Communion. Both rites are presented separately and are then put together so you can choose which ceremony suits the work you're doing or your personal preferences.

Both rituals, presented in their traditional form, are worded for group practice. However, if you are a solitary practitioner, you would simply act as the priest on your own behalf, and remove the "coven" parts of the ritual. Other modifications you may choose to make include Daemonic names used for each elemental blessing. You also have the option of switching Water West (instead of North) and Earth North (instead of West). There is a reason Water is North during this ritual, and Earth is West. There is an alchemical flow to the ritual that I'm sure even the most stringent magus is sure to appreciate.

With that I present to you the Abyssal Communion & Rite of Imbibement.

~S. Connolly

The Rite of Imbibement & Its Symbology

The Rite of Imbibement is rather controversial. It is a traditional ceremony in which members of the coven drink the blood of their coven mates. Now before you pass judgment you must understand the importance of this particular ritual.

To fully understand the Rite of Imbibement, one must understand the concept of the various parts of the soul. In particular, the Ib, or Heart. The Ib is the blood passed on from mother to child. It is the life force. This is why, in Daemonolatry, a magician who gives his blood in offering to the Daemonic or his coven-mates, even in small amounts, is giving something very sacred of himself. The blood is the life. The life passed from parent to child. Some have argued this actually means DNA. Perhaps, but we won't get into waxing philosophic here. Suffice to say this is, in part, why Daemonolatry is a blood-letting tradition and why blood is viewed as being so important. It is also the entire point behind Rite of Imbibement. Sharing something as sacred as the blood with one's coven is a bonding that has been practiced for centuries. However, unlike some human rituals where blood from wounds is mingled, in the case of the Rite of Imbibement, the blood of each participant, a drop or two from each, is mixed with some type of drinkable alcohol (which kills blood-borne pathogens) and is consumed by all members of the coven. What is not consumed is offered by way of libation to the Daemonic Divine.

We drink of our brothers and sister and share in the offering of their blood. Their blood becomes our blood. Our blood becomes all blood. The blood is the life. Praise be Sobek. For Khemetic Daemonolaters, Sobek is often called upon during the blood rite because the Crocodile God ruled the Nile of Egypt, the river that was Egypt's life blood. For Western Semitic Daemonolaters Sobek could easily be replaced with Leviathan, avatar of Yam. For more assertive Daemonolaters, substitute Lucifuge or Abaddon. For more feminine aspects consider Unsere, the great mother or Hekate, the triple goddess.

Within this book I shall use Sobek since I feel strong kinship with this Daemonic manifestation. Feel free to modify as your personal practice dictates. The Daemonic Divine does not find offense in modification.

Preparations for the Rite of Imbibement

The tools necessary for the Rite of Imbibement are minimal. You will want a ceremonial chalice, a ceremonial wine, and you'll need a bloodletting device. This device could take the form of a diabetic lancet, a pin, a ritual blade, or a razor blade. If using ritual blades or razor blades, heed caution. The safest, most sanitary method is a diabetic lancet device. Each participant can use his/her own lancet and the lancets can be disposed of in a sharps container. The alcohol of choice for this rite is traditionally a red wine. However, some people may choose brandy or whisky or even vodka. This is a coven choice. Red wine is usually palatable to enough for more people whereas harsher alcohols may take away from the rite. The wine itself serves as the base for the blood.

Prior to the rite, all participants should wash their hands with soap and water. The area from which blood will be taken should be as clean as it can possibly be. This is an important step to insure the purity of the blood wine and to minimize the spread of germs. The alcohol in the wine itself will destroy any pathogens within the blood.

Some covens may choose to use a special chalice specifically for this particular rite. Either way, the chalice should be clean and consecrated for magickal work. If you want to perform this rite in a very formal fashion, you would make sure to clean, clear and consecrate the chalice, the wine, and the blood-letting device(s) prior to the ritual or as part of the beginning of the ritual. This ensures that everything used is in proper form before the rite begins.

The rite can be performed solitary however you don't necessarily need to drink of yourself unless you are seeking to reconcile parts of the self, or as a symbolic gesture of drinking in one's own life. Some people do, others do not. Most, if not all, of the wine from a solitary ceremony will be offered by way of libation to the Daemonic Divine.

But since the coven based ritual is meant to drink of each other, all coven members must agree to partake. Those who choose not to participate should stand silently in the background with heads bowed in reverence. Those participating may stand near the altar or blood-letting station.

To modify the ritual for special circumstances, less formal tools can be used. The blood should not be mixed with any non-alcoholic beverage, but if it is, each participant must have his/her own cup or chalice containing the non-alcoholic beverage and each person should only imbibe his or her own blood offering (for safety reasons). The remaining blood-beverage should be offered to the Deamonic via libation.

In many modern covens there are recipes for the "Blood Wine" that may consist of various alcoholic concoctions. The following is one such recipe courtesy the Delaney Sect:

Blood "Wine" *Courtesy M. Delaney*
    Two Cups of Orange Juice
    1/3 Cup Tequila
    1 Shot Grenadine
    2-5 drops of blood from each participant.

Other covens will use other-than wine alcohols like Rum or Vodka straight. Ordo Flammeus Serpens keeps its traditional bottle of Hennessy Cognac in the temple for special occasions. All of this should illustrate how many variations and modifications you can make in your own performance of this ritual.

The Abyssal Communion & Its Symbology

The Abyssal Communion is a full elemental balancing ritual and acknowledgement of all the elements of creation both within and without. The ritual can be done as a ceremony by itself, or it can be part of a larger ceremony whether that Work is for worship or magick.

The communion does two primary things. First, it balances and grounds the participants in the foundation elements that sustain life. Second, it is a symbolic gesture of acknowledgement of the elements as all the elemental Daemons are invoked and each participant takes into themselves, each of these elements. This is also symbolic of nurturing the Daemonic Elementals within and without. It is during the invocation of water that the blood wine would be made, and the Rite of Imbibement done during the communion. To incorporate the rites is to declare all are one and one is all.

During the rite, each participant first takes in the air from the East, the essence of Lucifer's breath; the oxygen necessary to live. Then (s)he cups her hands around the flame to feel the warmth of the fire from the South. This is symbolic of the Sun and Flereous, the essence and avatar of Ra. Then each participant takes into him/herself a piece of salt atop a piece of bread, thus taking in earth, Belial from the West, who is sustenance; the nurturing element. Next, each participant drinks of water, Leviathan, the great serpent from the raging seas of the North. Water, in the ritual represented by the wine, is the blood of life and necessary for all life. Add to this the blood of our brothers and sisters and The Blood is the Life, Praise Be Sobek. So commences the Rite of Imbibement. Finally, each participant is anointed with the ceremonial oleum.

Together, as we take in these elements, we become whole and parts of the spirit and it becomes a part of us. We are never so grounded and balanced as we are when we partake of all of the elements, of the Daemonic, and feel each equally within ourselves.

Preparations for the Communion

    Initially it may seem the preparation for this Rite is rather elaborate, but once you've become accustomed to it, it will come together more readily each time the rite is performed. All participants, as with all rituals, should come to the temple bathed and clean. Whether they are robed or nude matters not, so long as each participant has purified him/herself. Having each participant drink a cup of purified water, and wash his/her hands before entering the temple is suggested regardless as both a symbol of internal purification and cleanliness of hands to handle the sacred sacraments of the ritual.

    For more formal communions, participants may be asked to refrain from sexual intercourse for at least 24 hours prior to the progression of the ritual. Fasting may also be practiced in more formal instances. However, neither are a pre-requisite for performing the ritual.

    Prior to the ritual the Priest or person performing the ritual must bring together the solar sea salt, the bread, the candle, the incense, the wine, and the anointing oil. All of these things and the vessels in which they will preside should be cleansed/cleared, and consecrated. Each elemental offering will be charged *during* the ritual. Be sure to have one large grain of salt for each participant (raw kosher or sea salt work best) plus five extra pieces of salt as offering to the Daemonic Divine. The incense should be a fifth element incense or a perfume significant of the spirit. Temple incense or a general purpose magickal blend, or one formulated for priests or priestesses are all ideally suited to the Abyssal Communion ceremony as many of them contain frankincense as part of the base ingredient. An incense of Lucifer is also acceptable. While making your own incense is the preferred method, purchasing an off-the-shelf blend is also acceptable.

If the Priest and/or coven are ambitious they can bake the bread themselves. This is also not required, but can add additional meaning, intent, and power to the rite. Likewise, the wine can be made especially for special Abyssal Communion or Rite of Imbibement ceremonies.

Like the incense, the anointing oil can be made by the Priest, or purchased off the shelf. I prefer an Abramelin or magickally centered oil. Some covens simply use *Red Tiger Balm* (1/8 cup) mixed with finely powdered Belladona (1 tsp), Cinquefoil (2 tsp), Mandrake (1/2 tsp) and Foxglove (1/2 tsp), which is essentially a flying ointment, though I'd take care not to get any near your mucus membranes unless you're using a safer, less stimulating base salve such as beeswax or cocoa butter. *Red Tiger Balm* contains menthol, camphor, cassia and clove, which will irritate delicate membranes, however it will stimulate the third eye, which is why some people have come to use it as an anointing oil for rites such as this. Hint: Try using it during meditation, prayer, or ascension practice for increased sensitivity.

Finally, any extra bread and wine will be offered to the Daemonic at the conclusion of the rite.

The Rite of Imbibement

It is easiest to set up a blood-letting station in the North quadrant of the temple. This way if the Rite is within the confines of another, the altar or station can be separate. At this blood-letting altar there must be the wine, the chalice, and the blood-letting devices (the lancets and discard/sharps container).

Those members of the coven participating should be sure to wash their hands thoroughly before the Rite. If the Rite is being done by itself, the temple can be opened standard (via Elemental circle), or in any construct the Priest or person performing the Rite sees fit. I am rather fond of performing this Rite within other Rites, and in this situation, you would simply perform your ritual as you normally would, and the Rite of Imbibement would happen in conjunction with request burning (since both require blood-letting) or prior to any closing offering ceremony.

So while the set-up of the initial rite is fluid and may change, the Rite of Imbibement proceeds as follows (solitary practitioners will play the part of the Priest and the group parts are eliminated or adjusted for solitary performance):

THE ABYSSAL COMMUNION & RITE OF IMBIBEMENT

PROCESSIONAL

The Priest approaches the North altar and lifts the chalice on high.

Priest: *By Nephthys we consecrate this cup for the sacred Rite of Imbibement.*

The chalice is placed back on the altar. The invocation seal[1] is traced in the air before it. The wine, which has been opened prior to the ritual and its placement on the altar, is poured into the chalice. The Priest again lifts the chalice toward the North.

Priest: *Before us the raging sea of the North brings the great serpent upon us! Bring with you blessings upon us! Praise be Leviathan, herald of Yamm.*

Coven: *Praise be Leviathan.*

The Priest holds the chalice in front of him.

Priest: *Brothers and sisters. Come forth and offer your blood unto Sobek.*

Coven: *Praise be Sobek. The Blood is the Life.*

One by one, members of the coven will step forward, take a lancet, and prick his/her own finger. Once a few drops of blood have been squeezed from the wound, the finger is dipped into the chalice of wine and moved around in the cup counter clockwise.

---

[1] See *The Complete Book of Demonolatry* for information on the invocation seal.

The Abyssal Communion & Rite of Imbibement

Priest: (after each blood-letting) *Your blood is our blood.*

Participant: *The Blood is the Life.*

Once all members of the coven who are participating have left their blood in the wine, the Priest sets the chalice back on the altar and adds his own blood to the Blood Wine.

The chalice is again lifted on high toward the North.

Priest: *Come forth Sobek! Bless this holy Blood Wine.*

The priest faces the coven.

Priest: *This Blood-Wine connects us all, and to all that is. Come forth, each of you, and drink of your Brothers and Sisters. Praise be Sobek, The Blood is the Life.*

Coven: *Praise be Sobek. The Blood is the Life.*

One by one, in procession from Major Adept to Initiate, each coven member steps up to drink from the chalice.

Participant: *I drink of my brothers and sisters.*

Participant drinks - usually just a sip.

Priest: (after each participant takes a drink) *Praise Be Sobek.*

Participant may make any gestures of his/her title/initiation or bow his/her head in reverence.

The Abyssal Communion & Rite of Imbibement

Participant: *The Blood is the Life.*

Once all participants have partaken of the Blood Wine, the priest then drinks from the chalice.

Priest: *I drink of my brothers and sisters. Praise be Sobek, the Blood is the Life.*

The Priest places the chalice back on the altar, traces the invocation seal in the air over it, and then proceeds with the ongoing ritual.

If there is no other ritual, all of the Daemons invoked for the ceremony are thanked and the ritual is closed standard[2].

MODIFICATION NOTES: This Rite can be done in the name(s) of Leviathan, Dagon, Yamm, Neptune, Poseidon, Hekate, Unsere, Lilith or any other Daemon (Divine Intelligence) ruling over water, blood or life.

---

[2] To learn how to open and close a typical Demonolatry ritual, please see *The Complete Book of Demonolatry*.

The Abyssal Communion

There are several ways in which you can set up your temple for this Rite. The first is to have a long table or altar in the center of the temple. You can use wall space along any wall of the temple if necessary. The second option is to use small tables or altars at each elemental quadrant within the temple. The first method confines the procession part of the ceremony to one central location in the temple. The second promotes a constant flow of energy and movement throughout the communion processional. I recommend attempting both methods at different times to see which one you're more comfortable with and/or which configuration the coven prefers.

A long table should be set up as such: On the far left, the incense burner with the incense. To the right of that, the ceremonial candle to represent fire. To the right of the candle sits the bowl of salt and the bread. To the right of that stands the ceremonial wine. Finally, the Priest or the Assistant to the Priest should be present with the oil to anoint each participant's third eye.

If you are using separate altars at each elemental quadrant the incense burner should be set up in the East, the candle in the South, the salt and bread in the West, and the ceremonial wine at the North. Once each elemental offering has been consecrated, charged and blessed by the Daemonic Divine, the Priest or his/her assistant should take his/her place at the center of the temple to anoint the third eye of each participant as the final step to the communion process.

If you're performing the Abyssal Communion by itself, the temple should be opened with a traditional elemental circle. For a Khemetic approach to this, see *Keys of Ocat*. For a standard approach, *The Complete Book of Demonolatry*. It would be redundant to repeat the information here.

If you are performing the communion as part of a larger ceremony, go ahead and open/construct your temple space in the manner most appropriate for the main ritual. If you are performing this Rite within the confines of another ritual, perform the Abyssal Communion just before any requests are burnt or offerings made and the ritual is closed.

Please note that if you are performing this ritual solitary, you would say the priest portions and modify the coven or participant orations/responses to suit your needs. This rite can also be performed in silence or while listening to music. There are many ways to modify it in ways personal to you. You can also choose different elemental Daemonic forces as you see fit to work with your personal pantheon.

PROCESSIONAL

The Rite should begin with the Priest approaching the East with the burning incense. The incense is held on high.

Priest: *O' Mighty Lucifer – Master of the four winds, bastion of enlightenment, hear me! I offer you incense for it is air we breathe and that which feeds the flames of our hearts desire. Bless this incense that we may take in its essence in honor of you. Charge this incense with your Divine breath. So be it.*

The incense is placed back upon the altar and the invocation seal is traced in the air over it. Then the candle is taken up and taken to the South (if you are using individual directional altars the communion items will already be located in their appropriate temple quadrant. You only need to take it to that directional quadrant if you're using a centrally located altar with all of the items upon it.)

The Priest holds the lit candle on high.

Priest: *O' Great King Flereous, Master of the Flame, herald of the Sun, hear me! I offer unto you the flame. This is the warmth we feel against our skin at mid-day. The spark of life and desire within. Bless this flame that we may take in its essence in honor of you. Charge this flame with your Divine desire. So be it.*

The candle is placed back upon the altar and the invocation seal is traced in the air over it. Then the Salt and Bread are taken up and taken to the West quadrant of the temple. The Priest lifts them on high.

Priest: *O' Great Lord Belial, Ruler of the Earth, the Root of Life, hear me! I offer unto you salt and bread, that which sustains us. That which nourishes us that we may thrive! Bless this salt and bread that we may take in its essence in honor of you. Charge the salt and bread with your Divine sustenance. So be it.*

The salt and bread are placed back upon the altar and the invocation seal is traced in the air over it. Then the wine (which has been poured into the chalice) is taken up and taken to the North quadrant of the temple. The priest lifts the chalice on high.

Priest: *O' Great Leviathan, Lord of the raging seas, the eternal soul and river of emotion in all things, hear me! I offer unto you this wine, the lifeblood of your creation. Bless this wine that we may take in its essence in honor of you. Charge this wine with your divine lifeblood. So be it!*

The wine is returned to the altar and the invocation seal is traced in the air over it. Finally the oil/salve is taken up and taken to the center of the temple space and lifted on high.

Priest: *O' Lord Satan, Master of the Abyss, Patron of the Spirit of All Things, and Great Ruler of the Infernal, hear me! I offer unto you this oil, the sacrament of the All. Bless this oil that we make take in its essence in honor of you. Charge this oil with your divine proclivity. So be it!*

The oil is then placed back upon the altar and the invocation seal is traced in the air above it.

Priest: (to the coven): *Come, brothers and sisters, partake of the elements.*

The priest then takes up the oil and stands ready to anoint each participant. In procession from Adeptus Major to Initiation, starting at the East, or left side of the central altar for the communion, each participant partakes of each element. If the altar is in one location, the participant simply goes down the line, taking in each element one after another. If you are using elemental altars, each participant will start at the East altar and work their way around the temple in a circle until they've finished at the North, then they'll be anointed in the center of the temple. In the latter construct, once a participant has finished at an altar, another participant can approach that altar. This is where the fluid movement comes in. When the altar is in a central location, it is polite to allow each person to finish his/her communion before the next person steps up to take theirs. First each participant breathes in the incense smoke. Then (s)he cups her hands around the flame of the candle to feel its warmth. Next (s)he takes a piece of salt and a piece of bread and eats it. Then (s)he drinks the wine. Finally, she approaches the Priest (or Assistant) and has her third eye anointed. Once finished, the participant stands aside in quiet prayer while the remaining participants finish the communion ceremony. As in all ceremonies of this nature, the priest goes last, finishing the Rite by thanking all Daemons present and closing the Rite standard. If the Rite is performed within another, this Rite concludes with thanks being given to each element, and the larger ritual is completed before closing.

MODIFICATIONS: Some covens incorporate a part to this ritual where the participants say: "Glory to Lucifer" after the incense, "Glory to Flereous" after they partake of the flame, "Glory to Belial" after taking in the salt and bread, "Glory to Leviathan" after drinking the Wine, and "Glory to Satan" after being anointed. Also "Praise be to [insert Daemonic name]." Also, in some covens a person my give the signs of his/her initiation at the conclusion of taking the Abyssal Communion.

The Rite of Imbibement + Abyssal Communion

The beauty of the rituals is in the rich symbolism of a combined Rite. Again, the combination can be performed as a Rite alone or within the body of a larger rite. As always, if incorporated in a larger rite both the Rite of Imbibement and the Abyssal Communion are done toward the end of a ritual just before the burnt requests and offering portion of the ceremony. Within larger rituals it is necessary to have at least two bloodletting devices for each participant. One for the Rite of Imbibement, and one for the Burnt Request/Offering portion of the rite. If you are only performing the Rite of Imbibement along with the Abyssal Communion, one bloodletting device per person should be adequate. Remember to practice safe, sane, and sanitary blood-letting.

In a combined Rite, the Rite of Imbibement, bloodletting portion, comes before Abyssal Communion, but the actual Imbibement portion of the rite is performed during the Communion itself. Again, be sure all participants have clean hands and fingers before beginning the rite. If you are performing the Rite by itself, construct the temple with an elemental circle. If you are performing the Rite within a larger ceremony, open the temple as necessary for that ritual.

Just as with the Abyssal Communion alone, the altar can be set up in one central location, or you can use altars at each elemental quadrant of the temple. You do need an altar at the North quadrant to facilitate the blood-letting portion of the combined Rite.

Processional

The Priest approaches the North altar and lifts the chalice on high.

Priest: *By Nephthys we consecrate this cup for the sacred Rite of Imbibement.*

The chalice is placed back on the altar. The invocation seal is traced in the air before it. The wine, which has been opened prior to the ritual and its placement on the altar, is poured into the chalice. The Priest again lifts the chalice toward the North.

Priest: *Before us the raging sea of the North brings the great serpent upon us! Bring with you blessings upon us! Praise be Leviathan, herald of Yamm.*

Coven: *Praise be Leviathan.*

The Priest holds the chalice in front of him.

Priest: *Brothers and sisters. Come forth and offer your blood unto Sobek.*

Coven: *Praise be Sobek. The Blood is the Life.*

One by one, members of the coven will step forward, take a lancet, and prick his/her own finger. Once a few drops of blood have been squeezed from the wound, the finger is dipped into the chalice of wine and moved around in the cup counter clockwise.

Priest: (after each blood-letting) *Your blood is our blood.*

Participant: *The Blood is the Life.*

Once all members of the coven who are participating have left their blood in the wine, the Priest sets the chalice back on the altar and adds his own blood to the Blood Wine.

The chalice is again lifted on high toward the North.

Priest: *Come forth Sobek! Bless this holy Blood Wine.*

The wine is then placed on the central Communion altar, or left on the Northern altar. Here begins the Abyssal Communion.

The Priest picks up the incense (if on a central altar) and approaches the East with the incense alight. The incense is held on high.

Priest: *O' Mighty Lucifer – Master of the four winds, bastion of enlightenment, hear me! I offer you incense for it is air we breathe and that which feeds the flames of our hearts desire. Bless this incense that we may take in its essence in honor of you. Charge this incense with your Divine breath. So be it.*

The incense is placed back upon the altar and the invocation seal is traced in the air over it. Then the candle is taken up and taken to the South (if you are using individual directional altars the communion items will already be located in their appropriate temple quadrant. You only need to take it to that directional quadrant if you're using a centrally located altar with all of the items upon it.)

The Priest holds the lit candle on high.

Priest: *O' Great King Flereous, Master of the Flame, herald of the Sun, hear me! I offer unto you the flame. This is the warmth we feel against our skin at mid-day. The spark of life and desire within. Bless this flame that we may take in its essence in honor of you. Charge this flame with your Divine desire. So be it.*

The candle is placed back upon the altar and the invocation seal is traced in the air over it. Then the Salt and Bread are taken up and taken to the West quadrant of the temple. The Priest lifts them on high.

Priest: *O' Great Lord Belial, Ruler of the Earth, the Root of Life, hear me! I offer unto you salt and bread, that which sustains us. That which nourishes us that we may thrive! Bless this salt and bread that we may take in its essence in honor of you. Charge the salt and bread with your Divine sustenance. So be it.*

The salt and bread are placed back upon the altar and the invocation seal is traced in the air over it. Then the wine (which has been poured into the chalice) is taken up and taken to the North quadrant of the temple. The priest lifts the chalice on high.

Priest: *O' Great Leviathan, Lord of the raging seas, the eternal soul and river of emotion in all things, hear me! I offer unto you this wine, the lifeblood of your creation. Bless this wine that we may take in its essence in honor of you. Charge this wine with your divine lifeblood. So be it!*

The wine is returned to the altar and the invocation seal is traced in the air over it. Finally the oil/salve is taken up and taken to the center of the temple space and lifted on high.

Priest: *O' Lord Satan, Master of the Abyss, Patron of the Spirit of All Things, and Great Ruler of the Infernal, hear me! I offer unto you this oil, the sacrament of the All. Bless this oil that we make take in its essence in honor of you. Charge this oil with your divine proclivity. So be it!*

The oil is then placed back upon the altar and the invocation seal is traced in the air above it.

Priest: (to the coven): *Come, brothers and sisters, partake of the elements.*

Now here is where the ritual differs because the Imbibement will happen AFTER the elements are taken in. If you are using a central altar, the wine is placed on the North Altar.

The priest then takes up the oil and stands ready to anoint each participant. In procession from Adeptus Major to Initiation, starting at the East, or left side of the central altar for the communion, each participant partakes of each element. If the altar is in one location, the participant simply goes down the line, taking in each element one after another (minus the wine!). If you are using elemental altars, each participant will start at the East altar and work their way around the temple in a circle until they've finished at the West altar (Earth), then they'll be anointed in the center of the temple. In the latter construct, once a participant has finished at an altar, another participant can approach that altar. This is where the fluid movement comes in. When the altar is in a central location, it is polite to allow each person to finish his/her communion before the next person steps up to take theirs. First each participant breathes in the incense smoke. Then (s)he cups her hands around the flame of the candle to feel its warmth. Next (s)he takes a piece of salt and a piece of bread and eats it. Finally, she approaches the Priest (or Assistant) and has her third eye anointed. Once finished, the participant stands aside in quiet prayer while the remaining participants finish the communion ceremony. As in all ceremonies of this nature, the priest goes last. Here we continue with the Rite of Imbibement:

The priest faces the coven.

Priest: *This Blood-Wine connects us all, and to all that is. Come forth, each of you, and drink of your Brothers and Sisters. Praise be Sobek, The Blood is the Life.*

Coven: *Praise be Sobek. The Blood is the Life.*

One by one, in procession from Major Adept to Initiate, each coven member steps up to drink from the chalice.

Participant: *I drink of my brothers and sisters.*

Participant drinks - usually just a sip.

Priest: (after each participant takes a drink) *Praise Be Sobek*.

Participant may make any gestures of his/her title/initiation or bow his/her head in reverence.

Participant: *The Blood is the Life.*

Once all participants have partaken of the Blood Wine, the priest then drinks from the chalice.

Priest: *I drink of my brothers and sisters. Praise be Sobek, the Blood is the Life.*

The Priest places the chalice back on the altar, traces the invocation seal in the air over it, and then concludes the rite by thanking all Daemons present and closing the Rite standard.

If the Rite is performed within another, this Rite concludes with thanks being given to each element, and the larger ritual is completed before closing.

MODIFICATIONS: Again, participants may say: "Glory to Lucifer" after the incense, "Glory to Flereous" after they partake of the flame, "Glory to Belial" after taking in the salt and bread, and "Glory to Satan" after being anointed. Also "Praise be to [insert Daemonic name]." Also, in some covens a person my give the signs of his/her initiation at the conclusion of taking the Abyssal Communion or partaking in the Rite of Imbibement.

An additional modification may include a less involved Rite of Imbibement where the wine is blessed and charged, but is taken in conjunction with the regular

Communion standard (see the Abyssal Communion Rite alone) and instead, before drinking each participant says "I drink of my brothers and sisters." (S)he drinks and then says "Glory to Leviathan. Praise Be Sobek, The Blood is the Life"

This eliminates the requirement of the priest to have to say anything so (s)he can focus on the anointing of each participant.

✷

So ends this liturgical sacrament in the name of the Daemonic Divine and the Nine Daemonic Divinities.
Amen.

~

𝔉𝔦𝔫𝔦𝔰

Notes

Notes

Notes

Notes

Made in the USA
Monee, IL
14 February 2021